LIGHT

AND

DARKNESS

RUSSELL SUSKO

©2020

ISBN (Print Edition): 978-1-66782-119-1
ISBN (eBook Edition): 978-1-66782-120-7

First Edition

Cover by Matt Davies.

Interior design/formatting by BookBaby.

Website: RussellSusko.com

Acknowledgments

Special thanks to those who helped make this book of poems a reality. My mother, Margaret

Pelepko Susko- editing. Matt Davies- cover design. Bookbaby- interior design and formatting.

Dedication

This book of poems is dedicated to my Mother, the kindest and most understanding person I have ever known. I am a writer because of your encouragement and praise. Thanks and love to you forever.

CONTENTS

SUMMER

REVELING IN SUMMER'S YOUTH

Sunburst
through dissolving morning mist,
dripping golden light
upon a meadow of wildflowers.
Rabbits running to and fro,
darting dragonflies avoiding capture,
monarch butterflies meandering about.

A damsel in yellow and earthy brown
looking into the blue above.
Curls of red hair bouncing
against bare shoulders as she spins.
Laughing, while her outstretched arms
play on the wind
which sings of an easy summer
just beginning.

A GARDEN SHARED

Lying in delicate flowers.
A song travels on the breeze,
so quiet,
floating like a whisper amongst the trees.
Mixed in, I recognize your voice;
your song trembles my soul.

Do you speak to me?
Do you sing for me?
Do you visit this garden, as I visit?

Your laughter and smiles planted
to bloom again in distant gardens.

BORN OF NORTH AND EAST WINDS

Born of Father,
bitter cold
with touch of frost, bite of ice,
and tears of snow

Born of Mother,
raging hot
with touch of blisters, bite of flame,
and bendless iron will

I am
of the forests, of the mountains, of the valleys and hills.
A soft voice rustling the leaves...
stronger now, rumbling through the trees.
At times, carrying voices and thunderous shouts.
Throwing boulders, plucking roots.
Wild...free

LOST AT SEA

LOST...Lost...lost

The horizon, a blue embrace of water and sky.
Hungry, starving, bones showing through.
Clouds overtaking, seabirds escaping.
Raindrops, Heaven's dripping dew.

Time is slow.
Time is weary.

Flame above and scorched below.
Skin of metal, bones of rock, blood as mud.
Heavy and heavier still.
Eyelids dipping, following the light
into darkness.

Sleep beckons.
Resist.
Struggle.
Alas...I have no more.
Alas...into the pall.

A PAINTING

Strokes of vivid light, thick as magma flows.
Brushed colors dancing over emptiness,
obscuring white.

Blurred images now in focus;
wispy clouds in the sky,
wavering grass and dense woods,
a garden in blossom.
Before a gate,
a woman looking over her shoulder;
black hair matching her mercurial eyes.

Meaning revealed, meaning hidden.
Meaning at all?

BROTHERS THREE

Three brothers, I the eldest.
Skin black, as the first ancestors of humans.
Smooth is my skin, brittle.
Beneath ground, of volume great.
Burn me.
Reborn in the air...
coughing, choking, smothering.
Coming for you

My brother, the second,
Brown as Mother Earth.
Skin smooth, sheen-less, liquid.
In the dark and the deep.
Burn him.
Freed into the air...
stifling, concealing, altering.
No escape

My brother, the youngest,
Clear as invisible vapors.
Skinless, shapeless.
Released from rock beneath the fold.
Burn him.
Escaped into the air...
diffusing, warming, overwhelming.
Run, flee, escape

To where?

TO HOME

Scattered stars like scattered homelands
torn apart, splintered and jagged
until countless pieces abound.
Streaking starlight smeared across the sky.

The sound- melancholy, haunting,
speaking my name.
"Today, tomorrow, all days were yours…now are ours."
Rhythmic melodies, the drums, the sirens,
the calls of battle, of war, of no return.

To home, I ache.
To bleed, I fight.
Such freedom contained within celestial bodies
not long beyond my grasp.
Always present, always reminding.
Home…no more.

I AM THE EARTH

Look at what I have given you.
The vast forests
breathing in death and exhaling life;
full of bark and leaf, root and flower, beast and bee;
given to ease your pain, cure your maladies,
provide your sustenance.

In return, what have you given me?
I see the genocide of my creation
with the axe, the saw, and the flame.
What I build
you knock down and uproot.
The friends I give
you slay for sport.
I smell the rot of your garbage.
I feel the burn of your pollutants, your chemicals
in my breath- the air,
in my saliva- the waters,
in my blood- the magma
on my skin- the earth.

Do you imagine that you can prevent me?
Build walls, and I will blow them down
with the tornado and the hurricane.
Build bunkers and impregnable fortresses,
and I will pull them asunder
with the earthquake- the opening of my mouth.

Flee in boats and face the gale, the tempest, the maelstrom.
Run to the highest mountain peak
to witness my tears flow,
sending the ocean to your door.

Accept me as I am
or suffer until I am remade whole.
I am death.
I am life.

Do you understand?
When I harm, it pains me.
The splitting of my skin, fracturing of my bones,
crumbling of my spirit.

Why do we share in this suffering?
Our fates are entwined.
If I perish, then I am the grave
of all life.

Do not look to my Red Brother-
cold as no winter humankind has felt.
Barren beyond the deserts you have walked.
More fruitless than any famine you have endured.
Breathless as space.
Lonely as the darkest corner.

You are my family.
I am your home.
You have no other.

OUR ROOM BENEATH THE STARS

Our hands held out a blanket
and on the grass it spread.
With gentle arms it welcomed
and gathered us to bed.

Surrounded in its warming,
it brought us heart to heart
that we might stay forever
and never have to part.

The night's breath caressed our skin
and smelled of flower bloom
until we thought of nothing
beyond our starry room.

NIGHT SONG

I sang a song into the night
and rang the bells of sleep.
Their voices called out names I've known
remembered in the deep.

Afar I peered into the gloom
into a silky sleep.
Solitude was the draught I knew
from cup of endless deep.

The time will come to drink no more
to dream upon my sleep.
Bring me comfort, bring me nothing
but leave me in the deep.

DEATH OF A STAR

Why this creeping fear of death
strengthening with age?

I cry aloud to the cosmos.
"What awaits me-
amnesia of bliss, of pain, of existence?
Is all forgotten?"

Look into the sky.
The darkness explodes in light.
A star raging, tearing,
splitting apart the night.

Ancient quantum knowledge released
in a scream
earsplitting as nearby thunder.

Give to me all memories the universe holds.
Spread your complete awareness
over my being,
so that I may shine as this dying star
in the colors of flame, of tropics,
pouring out from erupting wound.

Breaking, splintering, collapsing inward.
A star no more.
An incomprehensible void remains
full of celestial wisdom.

THE CLOTHES LINE

In the sun-soaked afternoon
below the bluest of blue skies,
a mother reaches up, wooden pins in hand.
Clothes dripping; drops running down her arms.

Looking out upon stretching green fields-
white dandelion seeds
caught in a gentle breeze,
floating like mist.

Before her, shirts flutter, flapping in the wind.
Sun upon her skin,
as she sings to the song birds.
Memories of children's laughter and little feet running bil-
low around
white sheets and wet linens; soft and warm.

THE LADYBUG

A ladybug sat on my nose.
I stared and stared 'til a thought arose.
Red and black halos drinking red and black dye
'til full, 'till fat.

The black disappeared in black.
The red sat on top its back.
One back in black all covered in dots.
The more I stared, the more I thought.

What if I was a ladybug all in black
with red upon my back?
Would I fly and land on a tree
or soar to a mountain peak from which to see?
Should I land on your nose or tickle your toes?
Maybe just smile and delight awhile
in the sun or the shade or the misty everglade.

THE FOX

Steeped in red and brown, trailed by white.
Black are my gloves and boots.
Stalking through shadows and digging holes,
scattering carcasses and bones without care.
Claws to scratch and rip.
Eyes like the void.

They call me cunning, sly,
self-contained, and shy.
They call me many things:
animal, hunter, predator.
But I am no fox,
for I was born of a higher species
with thoughts, contorted and anomalous,
and deeds, ruthless and nefarious.

Today, they have come
through forest deep and night unkind;
below a bright full moon
lighting their path.

Found and cornered am I.
Left staring down the barrel,
staring down
the end.

WATERS RISING

The sea lifted its head
and exhaled over our walls
of steel
of concrete
of sand.

It seeped between imperceptible openings
like opened doors.
And rose from beneath us.

Water rising, at our feet.
Rivers rising, flooding oceans.
Water rising…without end

LAVENDER TREES

Lavender trees, whose purple tears
frozen upon their boughs,
thaw in warm spring melodies,
basking in yellow glow.

Risen out of amethyst pools,
white buds like diamonds mined from starlight
open when sunlight kissed,
revealing in bursts their hidden color
and sweet fragrance carried on the backs of bees.

Their beauty beheld and cherished, but always fleeting,
relenting to the call of Time,
returning to the ancient garden
betwixt the Earth
and the resting place of forever.

THE RED SERPENT

Red twisting line,
a snake with mouth agape;
eyes white, fangs dripping venom.
Serpent slithers and climbs
over rock and root, dirt and grass
beneath a giant sun of morning.

Skin of scarlet red,
burning, drying, withering.
Seeks refuge on a tree.
Climbing heavenward, high upon the bark.

Betrayal bared.
Fangs sink deep;
venom flows, poison seeps.
Blood-tinged liquid diffuses,
flowing through bark, stems, and roots
like rivers.

Bark of brown changed to scarlet.
Leaf of green reborn in crimson.
The scarlet snake is drained, now empty and clear;
the tree now full and hyper red.
Slithers away.

THE ROPE

As a child, I possessed an unnatural fear
of string, cord, or a rope
hanging from above.
Seeing such a sight,
I trembled, perspiring in cold sweat.

As childhood elapsed,
my strange suffering eased
until at last, it was forgotten.
But destroyed, no, not so.
Buried deep and covered by mountains
made of time and pursuits.

But it was not to last.
Embers reignited,
bringing forth familiar fear.
Cold harbingers like cold water
sobering from sweet dreams.
But doom did not come, so in turn,
lax and bold I became.
The warnings lay dormant,
for I paid them no care.

In the world, I set out
in an unfriendly Age,
full of danger and doubt.
My enemies I crafted
masterfully and with great care.
Their vengeance came due, swift and final.
I hoped, I prayed, for my moment- deus ex machina.

But the rope still hangs, its hold is still tight;
its arms wrap around me, denying respite.
Hugging and hugging, my jealous companion
will not let go…will not let go.

ENCHANTED

Delightful smiles from eyes and lips.
Your words like butterflies
float light and smooth,
entrancing me without effort.

My eyes follow where you walk
captivated by your airy movements,
your graceful turns

My voice falters, searching for fitting words
to adore your beauty,
to express my boundless love.

My ears sing when you speak.

My heart leaps in your presence.

My thoughts aim at you
when you are away;
my consciousness slows
as movement in water.

THE WEIGHT OF LOSS

Into fog, into dreams, into...
escape- its succor welcomed.
Desperate
calls and shouts and screams
when no one can hear.
If only to be lost,
to escape my descending thoughts, my spiraling gloom.

What slakes thirst? What undermines hunger?
Simple physical relief could be procured
at a moment's notice.
Drink and eat.
But what relief conquers the foulest ailment?
This potent poison seeps through mortal flesh,
bonds with blood, engulfs the mind, and ensnares the soul.

Truest friend accused me thus
that fault lies with me,
"Occupy your time, for time
will let her go."
Noted my friend's advice, but my obsession grows.

Was it not I, who greedily accumulated your love?
Forewarned by common words,
"Until death do you part."

They say how we shall be,
"Reunited in Heaven's time."
But how long until then?
The weight of an hour
like weight upon my back.
Days carry *heavy*.
Months, years…
The bridge of time
long, forever long

TIME TRAVELER

As I could not be the amnesiac,
the man bereft of a past,
what else could I do?

Blackboards burning, seared chalk.
Equations read by most like hieroglyphs.
"Impossible," they said.
"He is mad," they said.
Impossible.

Weary, but I labor on
to discover my way
into the maze of time,
into the past, where I can save them.

My passion,
greater than the task

REUNION

Come to me
across time and space

Remember me
even when the worms of old age are fattened and full,
from feasting on your memories, their food

Look to me
my picture, your keepsake.
Joy and pain swirling together.
Longing…aching

Sing to me
over mountains and over storms;
when all can hear and when none are near

Cry for me
when tears are plentiful; when the past is at your door;
when you are lonely and afraid;
when hope is still

Come to me
when you are ready

A PEDESTAL INTO THE SKY

A garden in fall, lost beyond an abandoned house.
An overgrown path of stone
hidden beneath crunching brown leaves.
The gate wears a garment of vines.
Its lock fallen away, half buried in brown

Perfumes of autumn, of forgotten walks.
Memories of visitors who come no more.
Stone statues: the angels, the dancers, the tiger.
All obscured by wild growth, surrounded by twisted tree trunks
and leaves kissed by autumn's colors

In the garden's circular heart, looms the pedestal
encircled by marble steps spiraling above tree tops.
A breeze of air funnels up
to the platform standing on the forest's crown
awash in half-light

Here once, two lovers met
under starlight
in the inviting comfort of night,
walking in dreams awakened

THE MAIDEN OF DREAMS

Her eyes opened.
Therein, an explosion of
violet
tinting the twilit clouds and
falling like rain;
coating the days and
permeating the nights

I felt her touch
upon the wind
and then
she was gone

I closed my eyes
and saw her
in my dreams
within her gown of eternal promises
and radiant in all her smiles worn.
She brought the sound of laughter
light and delicate
with each of her footsteps

Her eyes met mine.
At once I knew her
and she knew me
completely and forever

I SAW HER FACE...IN THE SKY

From distance far, see, ever tall, the jagged mountain crown
sitting below colossal clouds puffy and still;
content to reign above, watching all.
A hesitant sun peeks over the mountain top,
throwing orchid pink and bittersweet orange
across the morning sky.

Memories of her voice
fill my ears.
Thoughts of our days of splendor
flutters my heart.

Her farewell words remembered dearly,
"On a morning clear, when the clouds sleep or hide away,
look to the sky and see my face, my smile, and my hope
that we shall be reunited soon."

My beloved kissed her fingers, and then toward the sky
released her love for me.
"This spell cast will not be undone
by anything less than this-
let wander your heart
and then free of me, shall you become.
When remembered, our love will burn,
and we will shine as the brightest stars in the highest skies,
undimmed by the darkest of nights,
baring all that we are and given
without reserve, without compromise,
and with all the joy we now possess."

This morning, into the sky I look,
as on all mornings since parting,
to see her face, to see her smile.
And I am full and bright, splintering and bursting.
My love pours out, sent forth into the world
to be with her
now and into the forever

SEA CLIFFS

From the bridge,
bracing against battering wind and chill,
I, the captain, watch
as the sea explodes-
salt sprays and burning cuts.

Into thick mist, drawing toward an ethereal world.
Siren calls from afar;
voices soft like mothers coddling babes,
promising weariness no more.
Heed their calls-
eternal mistake.

Through the mist as through a tumultuous dream.
Sunshine and warmth comfort with a welcoming embrace.
Wide cliffs loom in the distance-
sheer faces baring exotic colors
like the sands of the edge-of-the-world beaches.
The green atop beckons.

Once on land
to sea no more, for old bones do ache,
creaking and groaning.

Farewell sinking ship and exacting waters.
Our parting, though bitter,
cannot mar the precious memories
of this once young adventurer.
Now, all that remains is to sit
before a rousing fire and a goblet of ale,
telling stories to friends with eager ears.
Then, off to bed with treasured memories
to visit in the sleepy hours.

PATHS OF SAND

There are stone paths, windswept and fractured,
hidden in the desert sand.
Walk upon them and hear
the echo of ancient footsteps

Paths marked at their start by guardian pillars-
lion heads and bodies weathered smooth;
paws and teeth, fierce and warning;
eyes, all-seeing, wise, and unmoving

What do they guard and how do I pass?
Step forward- they watch.
Step again- hear a growl
low and deep like a waterfall's plunge.
Step once more- hear the breaking rock crumble;
see their hind legs move
and life flow through stone

Voices of thunder and earthquakes-
"Turn back adventurer. You are young and brave.
Do not squander such precious gifts," says the first.
"Turn back unwitting one. Only grim trials await," warns
the second.
"Or continue on to lands unknown and adventures plenty.
Expect not to return, wanting to or not," say both

Onward I go

THE PRISON CELL

What was once cool to my touch,
this metal brings no comfort now
in the growing heat.
These bars, these eternal sentinels-
blind and deaf to my supplications,
without mercy or pity,
without give or fatigue;
they are the perfect servants,
for they never fail.

Like an oven this chamber;
its heat ever rising;
its air so still.
The sweat drips and drips.
Still the metal is warm, tormenting me.

Come savior Night.
Pour your darkness over the land.
Blow your cold breath upon my room.
Fill me with shivers.
Allow me to sleep away
this oblivion.
Touch these metal bars
with your fingers
that pull away warmth
and make me forget the coming day.

SHE DANCES IN MIDNIGHT

I saw her
in the dim of night,
in its forlorn embrace,
beneath the pale glow
of distant and indifferent stars
caring not for what lays
beyond their spacial lands

I saw her
sitting on the loneliest bench,
waiting in the downpour,
so still and expectant.
Her eyes drawn to a window;
eyes entranced and full of hope

I saw her
when the window glowed from candlelight
and a child's face appeared.
Her smile was the summer's blossom
before the young maiden just betrothed

I watched her
rise and dance in Midnight's grace,
reveling in this precious time with him.
Her love shook the earth
yet the trembling went unfelt
I watched her
watching him.
His smiles, his eyes alive and bright brown,
unearthed her memories
once lived and yearning to live again

I watched her
in her Midnight Dance,
in soaked clothes reflecting the moonlight
as though she danced in her Kingdom of Mirth
far beyond this time and place;
where they await her return
beyond gates guarding golden shores
that her footsteps have known
and will know again

I knew her,

once, when she was a queen.

When her king held no power

and her prince was still hers.

When her heart lived between these midnight dances

and there was no desperation or despair.

When her child was still her child

and he was at her side.

When she held his hand

and his smile was her smile,

and his laughter was her laughter.

When she was his mother

and he was her son

SUMMER'S END HAS COME

Is this a dream
or an extraordinary enchantment
enwrapping my mind
with visions of a burning sun
brightening until bursting;
its internal liquid bounty
falling as molten rain

Luster of light and colors
surging through flowers,
leaves on trees,
dazzling skies, and regal birds
bound to earth and sky

Something has changed,
altering the vision.
Red emperors, helmars, and black tulips
melt and rain upward into the sky,
creating a colorful but turbulent mixture
like a painter's used palate

Close my eyes,
for if it is a dream,
then it shall be no more

Open my eyes
to a new land.
The sky is gray;
its color fallen
onto the wavering leaves
showing off their new raiment.
Dismal, meandering clouds rupture,
releasing rain

Fallen flowers like lost memories,
mixing in the mud

On the breeze is a slight chill;
it runs up my arms
and welcomes me
to a new season

FALL

THE LEAVES OF FALL

Green apples sour; green life fades.
The green leaves are turning
October orange, overcome by pumpkin's reflection;
sun-stained yellow, sublime in sunflower's borrowed robes;
ripened red, reflecting orchards' rubies.

Blown by Autumn's final breaths,
leaves of brittle brown crunch beneath feet;
battered, broken, and bound to the earth below.

PUMPKIN PIE

In a garden bright and green,
resting on a patch of grass;
body plump and lined with vine in hand,
the pumpkin is dressed in orange ripe.

Taken into proud arms;
muscles challenged by the weight.
Placed onto a table wooden brown;
its hat removed and belly hollowed out.

A warmed puree mixed in milky white.
Whiff of spice, cinnamon and cloves.
Baked in a delicious golden crust.

A LETTER ADDRESSED TO MANY

To false faces and mendacious minds,
To knowers and speakers of grave secrets,
you once welcomed me with handshakes and smiles
and then we parted with warm embraces.
Now, you are absent and troubled by coin counting alone.

To indifferent individuals,
To those same dealers of secrets, trading lives for gain,
you carried my mystery from avaricious and now absent allies
in haste and without consideration.
Now, you are returned home and welcomed by comfort.

To extravagant enemies and fawning foes,
To the most wretched of all,
you deal in death to the diminishment of the world
in haughtiness and convincing certainty.
Now, you are sitting and basking upon lofty heights.

To all who did betray,
To you now warned,
pay attention and be careful,
be cowardly, for the trap
is sprung!

WITHOUT WELCOME

Before the old mansion- sinister, mauve, and unmistakable,
see the haphazard hedges,
a leaning black gate and its slanted door on one hinge, objecting
to visitors,
bushes trimmed alive into grotesque faces,
a broken path of sunken stone and grass rising between cracks,
failing fountains, spurting muddied water,
the pock marked grounds- its holes deep-
and conspicuous metal traps- mouths open and teeth showing.

You see what I see,
yet you dare me to enter the grounds,
to ring the doorbell.
But do you not see
where I should stand on that porch
beneath the creaking chandelier
hung upside down?

The mansion's west façade of warped white
bares drip marks everywhere.
The rooftop corners occupied by watchers;
gargoyle lookouts with faces half man, half beast,
bloodied tongues across cheeks, eyes piercing and hungry.
A metal chimney shaped as a raven's claw; talons pointed
and sharp.
Chimney smoke- gut green and banished black.

A cloud made of swirling crows
whirling wildly in madness.
Descending, its dark shadow and dreariness
pervade the grounds like a pestilence.

Sign upon post
planted at the foot of termite-feasted steps.
Its words clear:
Death or Doom to those who knock.

THE LEAF

Whispers and echoes in the darkness
Tremors and vibrations and nothing still
A rupture, a spreading fissure
Light awakens movement
Reaching
Escape to freedom

In darkness, doused by rain
Dried by light
Bud forming shape
Veins amid a green sea
Surface smooth and fleshy
Jagged edges
Swaying, rocking, wind-touched too
Changing, turning

Memories of green, reality of red
Hanging
Browning

Falling

Crunching too

THE GIRL WITH DANDELION HAIR

Paper birds and wooden frogs
resting on a marble floor
far beneath a dome weaved of tree limbs.

Bookcases reaching; their company packed tightly on shelves.
Books with green bindings and curving yellow runes
All kept safe behind a door of etched silver
which opens
and in steps a girl
fair and wise,
her hair of dandelion, her face aglow,
her words are fluttering, their powers of old

Before the sun sets, she begins to sing.
And when she dances,
the paper birds will fly
and the wooden frogs will leap

A STRANGER IN MY HOUSE

I am but a ghost,
a living memory, an echo of a voice,
a vibration of movement,
worse than an illusion.
I am invisible.

My love moves in sorrow, floating through tears.
My whispers stir her dreams.
My touch softens her loneliness,
but life repels the dead.
I cannot linger.

Into the garden, into nature.
Give her time.
Give her space.
I cannot go far,
not for long; she pulls me back.
I feel her longing, tearing at the boundary
between us.

Time is relentless.
I am fading, slowly, but I know.
She grieves less, swims less through her memories.
From my clothes, my scent fades
from the sofa, from it all.
My voice has softened.
My footsteps are lighter than air.

Two years gone;
everything is fainter.
There is a stranger in my house.
She and he are together
more and more.

My pictures are in drawers.
My clothing all in boxes.
Look at me; am I like the night's light-
ethereal and dwindled?
Soon I shall be gone.
When she has put
the last of me away,
and only memories remain,
ghost I shall be no more.

THE PATH OF LEAVES

Leaves of all colors,
blowing in the howling wind,
rush past my feet
over a stone path flecked with black,
leading to an ancient arch
marking the way
into an old-growth forest of profound age
from whence none return

Where does it lead?
My mind cautions but my body is entranced.
My strong footsteps announce my coming-
tap, tap, tap, tap.
The turbulent wind blows fiercer,
gripping my clothing, gripping my skin,
pulling me from the path.
I struggle against the fury, leaning into it

At the threshold,
curve of the arch directly overhead.
Strength waning, doubt creeping in.
The wind ceases.
Fallen onto my stomach into the soft, leafy catch.
An unseen gate slams shut somewhere behind.
Welcome, says a voice

WHITE WITCH

A witch of good called witch of white
can be found behind a veil
made of petals, mist, and brighter things
and formed by a powerful tale.

She receives no visitors aside from me
in her cottage set beneath a giant tree.
If my tale so far sounds too good to be
and you are full of incredulity
then satisfy my gentle plea
and come along as company.

Who am I? Well, no one you can see,
but today a friendly guide to accompany thee.

We will open her door
to aromas of fall, of sugar and spice.
See therein
the dried leaves and wooden wind chimes;
green apples dusted brown,
potted plants and carven figures
on tree-bark shelves open to view.

Go to the windowsill, to the pumpkin pie steaming.
Look out on smiling green-eyed cats, prowling the yard.
And butterflies walking on flowers, watching her door.

Singing sweet songs whilst brooming the walk,
the white witch is happy,
for the deep night will carry the full moon.
The time to fly is near;
not upon closet broom but on tree limb smooth;
its rings, its stories, too long untold.
But the night will bare them, let them unfold.

For now, she sweeps,
with her hair like autumn's golden leaf,
untied and flowing.

THE WITCH'S LAIR

Within a furnished cave
musty, dusty, and bleak,
gloom weaves with shadow;
depression inlays in stone.
Scents of despair like scents of flowers,
poison one's spirit.
Dead things like decorations-
some are littered about
while others are placed with considerable care.

Eyes ever watching, hidden from sight.
Hands ever grasping, eager and ready.

Voice of scratches and smile of rot.
Do not look into her eyes,
those eyes without escape.
Do not listen to her terrible words,
words that should not be spoken.

Stay far away, stay always away,
for once inside,
she is your host
for a lifetime and a day.

FLAMING LEAVES

A forest's dark under vanished moon.
Unnatural silence, stillness,
and absence of life.

Explosion of sound.
Explosion of heat.
Burning orange light flickering from smoke-
flaming leaves charring and crackling,
twisting brown, singeing black.
Carried on the wind and gathering together,
massive pile of acrid ash.

Dim white light protruding, escaping the core;
more brilliant still, growing and spreading.
A pile of solid light, its shell cracking, opening.
Life emerges.

A HAUNTED OCTOBER SKY

Can it be?
An orange sky in late afternoon
as though the sun had exploded,
throwing itself over the world's roof
like a pumpkin smashed apart.

Dark shadows in the distance,
ominous and unnerving, stretching as phantoms.
The nearby trees without leaf or friend
except for visiting bats and owls.
Their hard limbs creaking in the cold;
moved by an austere wind, impatient and old.

Breathing in the scent of leaves mixed in dirt,
I hide behind a rough wizened tree.
Ever so far from home,
waiting in this dull, lonely place
unvisited and unwanted.

The hour has come
and the light is changed.
The sky!
The orange is thick, almost overwhelming.
My skin dances in prickles and shivers.

Look at the shadows joining hands,

blending together,

stretching tall and wide;

they are now one.

A castle of nightmares stands where none had been

upon a slanted hill

at the end of a muddy path

clustered with shriveled brown grass.

Its windows look- eyes alight and glowing.

Its door opens- mouth of sharpened metal teeth.

Its rusted gate swings- voice harsh and repugnant.

But I will not go,

for no fool am I.

Stay here, stay here and hide.

THE LANGUAGE OF SNOWFLAKES

Yesterday,
the leaves were wet and brown.
Today,
they are no more
on the trees.
Laid to rest on rich dark earth,
a wet crunchy grave.

The clouds overhead, once white,
are now grim and gray
and sing of distant lands of ice.
Harbingers of change;
whispers of a piercing cold
pervasive and deep.
Heavy layers of darkness and lingering snow,
coating and covering- a reimagining of all
in crystal and white.

In the snowflakes is a pattern;
it's a language
from the forgotten frosted hills.
On each, a word is written;
seen together is a story.
Can you see it?
Can you read it?
Try in the soft moonlight.
Hurry, for upon landing,
the words bend, break, and melt,
forming a pool of ink
to be raised and rewritten
by the season
that is Winter.

WINTER

THROUGH THE ICE

Aboard our vessel in the icy mountains,
sailing amongst the clouds.
Cocooned in fur, gifted by bear of Polar region,
we stand around a fire
raging in a metal pit.
All at once, the deep cold confronts us.
Breathe out the chilling air
frosting before my eyes,
whose touch is like a grave hand.

Through the clouds, the mist,
the breath of passionless Creators.
Our movements slow, our breathes heavy.
How long until journey's end?

At my side, my kin, wanderers
cast out from a known land warm as the sun is bright,
fresh as the forest is green, firm as the earth is strong.
Distant, lost, never to be, never to be home again.

In these clouds, the swirling mist is a waking dream,
luring our vessel deeper
and deeper into a confusing maze,
from which they say all are lost.

Then I feel it; the touch of my beloved,
delicate as a flower's petals.
But in that touch, concern, uncertainty of the future,
longing for the irretrievable past.
Look. Eyes meeting old friends, unshakable, inseparable.
In those bottomless dark depths
finer than night sky,
filled with deepest blue,
is visible a lifetime of moments precious,
passions shared, and hopes formed and lost-
some taken and some given,
given away with tears and full hearts.

But this is our world and our time.
These are our choices and destiny spinning faster,
gathering tighter until they burst.
"We are almost there."
"I long to be planted again."

And then it reveals itself.
Great cliffs, marble clad in pink and blue,
against the dusky autumn sky.
Climb. Climb to great heights.
We shall; up massive green vines woven into stairs.
To a fortress on a plateau, whose garden is the sky.
To walk across the Bridge of Glass
over waters of crystal and ice...

THE BIRDS UNSEEN

There are these birds of green.
I see it in their eyes;
they are watching and they know
about mysteries, secrets,
and things that go untold.

Here they stop
and here they stay
but noises make they?
Nay, for they are silent,
always silent.

Their coats, covered by winter's cold,
speak of a time and of a place
and of a power of the old.

I shiver, they watch.
I whisper, they hear.
But do they speak?
And do they think?

Do they notice that I stare
with my mind's aim upon them?
To enter their minds' maze
and turn their cogs.
To fly as they may
through the dreams of that Age
when they walked upon the land
and none stood so tall;
when such as they beheld
nothing, oh nothing,
but magnificence unlulled.

BLEAKNESS BY DAY

Deeper than the darkness of night.
Deeper than the gloom of oblivion.
Dusting despair over all

Waves of sadness crashing around me
Coating over sounds and thoughts,
Deafening, paralyzing

Escape
But moving pulls me backward, downward
Into heavy darkness, into heavy depths
Funereal depths, slowly sinking…sinking

Scream
But stifled by an icy, lifeless hand
Covering my mouth
Gripping, pressing, nails biting

Shake
My head clear
And put away these thoughts.
"Smile, for it will get better,"
They say

BLEAKNESS BY NIGHT

Bright lights smeared, distorting faces and smiles.
Friends merging into strangers.

I
do not look at strangers,
for they are monstrous
with slinking, twisting tongues
and sunken teeth, eyes protruding, flesh enflamed.
My broken sight sees shadows through splinters.

I
reach for oblivion, feeling its edge
palpable but rough, cold, and formless.
It pulls and pulls hard;
bites and clamps down.
Let go
Freed from its grasp.
Alas, it never lasts.

I
hear their voices like wet gravel
grinding together;
a contortion of screams and lies.

I
stumble in the dark,
rolling until disorientation sets in.
When I sit up, I am in a decayed garden
in full bloom.
Effervescent glow of cobalt blue
set before the complete darkness behind.
Therein, I see darker things;
shapes moving against the darkness.

I
breathe in the gray vapor
rising from a rotting, muddy floor.
It smells of the tomb, burning my nostrils,
invading my mind,
clouding it with wretched forms.

I
close my eyes
and wait
for the light.

HIDDEN PATH, HIDDEN REALM

Part the mist of violet
To reveal a hidden realm
The splendor of a garden
The splendor of a crown

To play the air as a harp
And unlock a mystery
To walk on a hidden path
And come as you are free

I heard the stories long ago
In the cold of Winter's eye
I thought them as a kind of lie
Those whispered by the old

Know I now, that it is true
Know I how to fly
Into a river without time
Into the most sublime

Time stops not for you or me
Nor any that I know
For time was never of this world
But neither, now, are we

WHAT LIVES IN THE LAKE?

Mist creeps out
from the dark lake shore
through the thickening gray of afternoon,
and crawls over sharp-edged stones in black and brown,
resting on mossy beds.
The air is cool like my brow
in the pervading stillness.

What will rise today
from the liquid murk,
from where bubbles rise?
Ageless runes led me here;
the characters dark upon a silver tome.

The water parts like my courage.
Ethereal light rises in tunnel form.
A voice, a creature.
Running am I
far and fast away.

BLACK BIRDS

Birds seeped in dark of night,
dressed in obsidian-feathered coats
dipped in an inky pool.
Dripping and flapping wings
throw gloom over the mountains
and across the sun,
blotting out light.

They
muddle the wind with foulsome odors,
hunt prey with ravenous delight,
give no quarter to those below.

Seeing far and seeing small.
Seeing you, in the rock's shade.
Seeing you, beneath blade of grass.
Riding on the folds of wind.

THE SHADOW AT HIS BACK

What dark secrets
lay in the shadow at his back
watching,
waiting,
willing him to speak,
wanting to speak their own

No refuge, no escape.
Not another day…*today.*
Truth laid bare.
Lies scorched by morning light.
Voices loud and clear.
Monstrous deeds and terrors

Light, light upon shadow

HOW SWEETLY THEY COME
FOR EVERYTHING

They speak to me in words
so sweetly dressed in sugar;
hung by hope of cruel intent,
espousing pleasant times tomorrow.

But I do hear something else;
it's the crunch and grind of gravel;
it's the true intent, the viper's hiss,
the strike and sting and sorrow.

They smile at me, their expressions invite
all the comfort their concerns can carry.
With a smile, with a nod, it's easy to see,
see how their eyes do sparkle.

But I do observe something else
that looks like a mask of putty.
It's old, it's dry, is it simply to hide
the face behind that's molding?
Or is it something else like the end of lies
and the start of truth, its telling.

Truth shall shine to all the knowing
shine and shine forever showing.
As born was I to see and hear
and know what you are knowing.

THE CLIFF PATH

Here I stand
atop a narrow path of stone
without fissure, crack, or chip.
On my left, an unforgiving fall
into sea green and grim.
On my right, a mirror image
of this two-sided cliff.

Long is the walk to a prison castle.
Its stone in constant shadow.
Ominous is the air above its walls.

My love, by rock and metal bar encaged.
Chains upon flesh, bar across door.
Guarded by monsters living and dead.
The cursed, the condemned, the evil reborn.

Come has the wind's wrath
and the sea's spray
mixed into bitter brew
battering against my body.

One look, into the final fall,
one look, upon them with sunken eyes,
discolored oozing flesh,
and stone-piercing claws,
climbing higher and nearer
up the cliffside.

Pelting rain from dismal clouds.
Unnatural lightning flashes
in vermilion and putrid orange,
illuminating dreadful, haggard faces
staring down from the angry sky.

Dread of what is still to come.
Dread of failure and of these eyes
looking never again
on my beloved wife.
Dread beaten back,
to be taken up
by someone
lacking my unwavering heart.

Into storm, into fury.
Forward, Forward

CHANNEL OF LIGHT

Barefoot upon the rings of Saturn
on imperceptible dust
on smooth, cratered rocks
on frigid ice

Beams of light.
Perfect silence, until
an unknown voice calls me forward

The rings pulsate-
brilliance grows, explosion.
Beacons and radiant upside-down waterfalls;
a golden mist, untouched and unfelt.
Reaching up into infinite sky.
Lost in light, dissolving, conjoining.
Now one

EXOPLANET VISITED

Lonely darkness, untouched and undisturbed
Visited not, forgotten not
Sharing space with starlight

One spaceship fallen through singeing atmosphere
Burning, reducing, existing still
Landed on alien soil

Methane lakes, noxious fumes
Rain of glass
Rain of diamond
Falls and falls

WORLD OF MIDNIGHT

A planet without motion;
its one eye upon starlight brilliant;
its surface scorched giving no relief

The other eye looking
upon darkness deep, silent,
and broken by one barren rock- one moon;
its cool reflected light cast down below

From sunlight's side,
warmth
flows to moonlight's side,
flows to cities upon cities

Midnight gardens, conversations and song;
a world forever awake in midnight's hour

WINTER LEFT IN THE NIGHT

The night changes all
even with a single passing.
Put out the roaring fire
that once pushed back the stubborn cold.
Put away our blankets
all fluffy in cream
and our spiced tea,
rich and comforting,
that we once savored
in funny little cups
dripping honey
from curling slender mouths.

Put away somber loneliness
and empty dark thoughts.
Step beyond the threshold
and breathe the new air.

Gone away, the frosted breath
and the unmistakable crisp air.
Frozen earth thawing,
wet with the smell of new life.
Fallen is the old world
to be no more.
Risen is a new world
resplendent and green.

SPRING

WAITING FOR THE RAIN

Rain, when do you come?
Tomorrow? Or on another day?
Why not come now?
Do you hear my call?
Yes, it is me.
This is *my* voice calling to you,
breaking through the hot thickness
like rising steam spreading
over the land
and over me.

In the distance,
I see lumbering gray clouds like sky fortresses,
perfuming the breeze,
tingling my skin, raising my hairs.

When last you fell, piercing the gloom,
you were miserly, slaking no thirst;
when through parting clouds, the strengthening sun
dusted you in dream-like golden light;
you stopped falling and hid again.

I am but a bird.

But am I not worthy of you?

Shall I ascend to your lofty height?

In flight, follow

through darkness deep and foreboding,

through breath blown from Godly lips,

through lightning's flash and thunderous roar.

Pity me and come soon

or no friendly face, no sweet melody to meet

just bones…and a memory.

THE BLOOMING OF THE BUD

A bud of green grew out of grass
and cherished in the dew.
The sun shone down to kiss the ground,
then all the sparrows flew
above the trees into the height;
they sailed on a cloud.

The bud broke through in buttery blue
and stood above the crowd.
The bees buzzed by, yet one did try
to shade in petals wide.

We saw the hand reach out and pluck
and all at once we cried,
"There once danced too, a bud so true
it forced upon a smile.
Yet we shall wait for its twin mate
no care how long awhile."

PATH OF MIST

A public park glossed by morning light.
Still…empty.
Quickened pace, exit the square.

A walkway of cobbles sided by fashioned shrubs
shaped as arrows pointing.
Leading me where?

The thrilled beating of my heart at such unknown.
Deeper go, until mist-covered gardens show.
Intense green, dripping dew, swirling mist.
Quickened pace, echoed footsteps.

Something beckons…something awaits.
The cloud thickens, enclosing.
Trapped, blinded by cool white.
Pricklings of fear, of mistrust.
One guide beneath my feet.
The path leads on.
Follow, I must.

At last…the end.
Weathered arch of stone
draped by vine and ivory.
Once hidden, but no more.

Curiosity's hand, warm and tender,
leads me where?

I BELONG ELSEWHERE

My home was never really my home.
Beautiful, yes.
Blue and white like deepest, coldest ice;
cascading water with strength of centuries behind.
Daybreak splintering as the glass rainbow;
hyper-violet hue splashing over orange dawn.

But more than sight.
Smell the rising blossoms
full of the night rain and the morning star.
Taste the soil's rich bounty.
Hear the Earth's breaths as it turns
and the call of wild birds holding the back of the wind.

But it does not feel like home.
It never has.
I belong elsewhere as do some of the sun's rays,
shining past Earth, traveling far into the cosmos.

BIRTHDAY

365 turns into darkness, into light.
Turning around our star,
hula hooping at 66,659 miles per hour.
A turn of the seasons

Breathe in Spring.
Mixed of rich dark earth and dew-sprinkled grass;
violet petals dipped in mild winds
and softened in sunlight

Hold in Summer.
The volcanic-orange bloom
drenched in pelting rain, misty shrouds and halos

Exhale Fall.
Your leaves changing raiment.
Gusty temperament, chilly embrace,
scent of farewell breaths

Breathless Winter.
Wrapped in white-sapphire ice and welcome cold.
Known for ages.
Known to slow and darken.
But bringing us together,
promising a new turn, a new year

AGING

Slow as the turning years
Unnoticed as the shifting continents
Unseen and unfelt in the moment
Until its results are unmistakable
Not in hours, not in days
But patiently, hour by hour, day by day
Through years and through decades

Endless possibility once
Now
Rigid lines of a known path
Fond memories swirling, fading
Some forgotten

A moment of desperate hope to live again
Declining into grave acceptance
Fritter away in despair what little remains
Or revere the emptying hours
The closing of the cycle

INVISIBLE LINES

A world of chaos, a world of strife.

Borders everywhere.

Man-made contrivances, man-made walls.

Separated

by mountains and seas,

by color- my skin,

by sound- my language,

by the intangible- my ideas.

The lines between countries

parallel

the lines between us.

HUMANITY'S WAR

Fallen ash from sky above.
Horizon orange, flickering.
The Earth's skin trembles.
Man-made sorrows and their siblings, Death and Doom.
The cries.

The taste of bitterness, floats on acrid air.
Where once was laughter and voices
Now
Only silence, disturbing and unwelcome.
Accursed ground, withered and warped
Beneath the bone-dusted landscape.

Starlight turns away.
The night shudders in anger.

Cracking, a splitting from Pole to Pole.
The world opens; its lifeblood spills out.
Liquid core runs like yoke,
Covering, smothering,
Burying all

But dawn awakens as it must
To hope and to new life

GHOST BEFORE ITS GRAVESTONE

I feel it in the cold air.
I see it in the star-touched night.
I hear it in the early hours.
Traces of an ancient past-
reverberations of footsteps and laughter
subtle until tonight,
for I hear them now,
strong and clear as a beating drum

Who were you?
Who are you?
Moss-speckled stone before the mountain,
familiar as yesterday.
Its blank face betrays
no name, no memory
of the one buried beneath

Who am I?
Who was I?

GRIEF'S MIRAGE

To be drunk from the spring of bitter tears
whose misty-eyed draught hazed the senses
and perfumed the brain with mirages
touched by enchanted colors and visions of beauty
animated by the meeting of the Sun and the Stars
dripping eternal drops of Heavenly nectar
soaked up by goddess-walked earth
and giving birth to wild green
drenched by the river-dipped hair of Mother Wind
and blooming into infinite hues of light-drinking petals
bearing the insect, with twins anon and forever,
spit out by bird of particular palate
and claimed by fish
smiling beneath the separation
of those below
from those above

TIME WILL NOT SEPARATE

The first time I looked upon her face-
explosion of memories and haunting emotions
once hidden and safe;
buried in a vault beneath mountains
and oceans of fathomless depths.
Now, released as typhoon-tossed water.

The first time I saw her was not the first,
not the first but nearer the thousandth time.
No, greater still, for thousands and thousands pale
before the lifetimes we have shared.

Awaken heart.
Release my ancient love born upon the dawn of days
when she and I were strangers not
and loved as the flower loves the morning dew.

My heart calls to me in its beating:
Tell her…Tell her…Tell her.
O, I desire such, beyond the measure of words
as none have wished for, even in their obsession profound,
even in their jealousy of roaring fires and magma glow,
as though all the world was consumed in this one thought alone.

But alas, I cannot,
knowing of the terrible reward,
for to speak of the secret
brings oblivion of all,
wiping away precious memories
of when we passed
through wind-swept fields below rising peaks
touched by ruby-crowned kinglets' breaths and snowshine;
when we strolled through meadows
full of craning wildflowers beyond the water's fall
where our hands met in floating dances,
and we received heaven-sent kisses
that were smiled upon by the faeries
sprinkling the dust of joy upon our crowns
with each of their laughs,
as they twirled and twirled through the days.

Today, we are strangers no more,
for when our eyes met,
I saw in them the reflection
of all of our shared memories.

THE PRISONER

Carrion birds whispering death
have come to visit me.
In black complete, they wear the night
and know about the tree
where I shall hang out all my days
and wish that I was free.

Never nearing, ever staring,
watchful from afar.
Their grim intent is kept at bay
by bendless iron bar.
Here they perch and here they patter
to squawk away the rays.
What gruesome guests I have today
but dare I not dismay.

My view, my torture, be it not so
keep not the world away.
My friends and kin did weep alike
their tears could no one sway.
But they have gone and not returned,
so think of them I do.

Here I shall wait with friends no more
and nothing else to do
then listen to chattering birds
before I bid adieu.

THE LIGHT AND THE GREEN

Awoken to a morning
of rich dark green
drooping and dripping
from an early rain.

Full and heavy
giant gray clouds
hold back the light
of the heavenly gem.

Inhale a fullness, a richness
of sky-rain and misty white
stretching across the mountainside.
What secrets lay behind?
What opulent doors
of earthy wood
inlaid with glimmering metal
and words of natural power,
open to faerie gardens
and worlds of beauty
beyond our known plane of existence?

All at once,
the sun reveals itself;
its brilliance
mixing with the wet green
like liquid yellow diamond and crystal
running down, dripping from emeralds.

SUMMER

A STAR LOOKED DOWN

"My daughter, look out upon the vast and the emptyless.
See our ancestors' eternal glow
lighting the pathways of mortals
who journey between the plane of creation and of eternity.
But look not down,
for to watch the mortals is to become like them."

Remembered my Father's words, but followed them I did not.
Across darkness forever flowing, my gaze did fall
upon swirling whites over placid blue,
through thick mist
to the glow of morning
rising upon mountains high and green-swept lands
abundant of stark beauty singing through the hills
into peaceful homes warmed by kind words-
flawless in feeling as the overflowing hearts of the Creators.

Since the start of the time of stars,
my eyes did not wander
until they set upon that world.
That which holds the universe together
tired of my star
and sent me down
to walk upon the Earth

THE CURSE UPLIFTED

Before your eyes were open,
before you knew laughter and exchanged smiles with us,
before voices became familiar and you felt a comforting embrace,
a stranger's fury designed a curse
born to be placed upon your brow.

You were
raised in comfort to much delight
but guarded and sheltered and given no flight.
Upon the welcome age, the search began-
a suitor to find, a spiteful curse to break.

For years, all who looked upon your face,
in repulsion and disdain, did howl and flee.
Until a day, when one came, who stood oblivious to ridicule
unmoved in the hurricane,
entranced by your eyes, frozen to your gaze,
warmed by your smile.

A kiss of love, a kiss of truth-
uplifted the curse, freeing you.

Not long thereafter, on your wedding day,
the dull clouds parted,
and the charming sun smiled on our garden
and on you, in full bloom.
Red dahlias and snapdragons reflected off your white gown.

Our smiles spoke true of future days
of great promise.

LEFT BEHIND

My feet touched upon earthly rock
whilst you laid down
upon a bed of heavenly cloud.

You left me,
taking with you
not my love,
nor my heart,
nor my memories
of you.

PLAGUE

The smell of rotting meat under a stifling sun,
floated upon the breeze creeping under doorways
and seeping through imperceptible cracks in the window pane.
Perfumed masks in black,
sculpted into the likeness of a bird's face,
but none of it worked, as more of them fell,
sickness, sickness for all.

Retreated to sanctuary, for our mother did say,
"The plague is coming, so we must away,
far and far behind lengths of green,
beyond gate and wall, beyond a castle's thick stone."
There we went but short was our stay.
Again, plague had come, so again, we went away.

Returned to coughing city streets overwhelmed by fear,
for many walked hand-in-hand with death
which all feared.
No relief for the marked; their skin was aglow
in the shadows, in the alleys, we heard their constricted
breaths blow.

Touched once by pestilent lips, by my love
whom I could not but hold
until all I embraced was nothing but cold.
The shivers, the shivers, relentless and unlulled.

Held down was I by invisible chains;
their weight insurmountable,
and was it not plain
that their keyholes were lost,
were lost, were lost.

I heard my heart quieting below my fading breath,
so I asked,
"Why my heart, beat you less and less?
Heart! Do not knock less upon my chest,
for I wish to live
and death is all but untrue."

They have come all
to gather at my side.
In the end,
I have only these words to say,
"Look not upon me those that I love,
for I can be with you no longer, here above.
Remember when we laughed,
even when we cried.
But above all remember, when we are no more together
that once we held the wonder…of the rising day."

WHITE

Minions of the white death
miniscule under microscope but potent.
Infecting and conquering,
turning flesh pale and cold.

Confused, lost in mist or clouds.
White vapors to breathe when death be sought.
Smooth growth twisted, infected by white worms.
Into the desert, a white wasteland withholding drink,
burning and leaving pallid scorches.

Blinding light emitted from a pale sun.
The boredom of white space and white walls.
Breathing in white powder, the endless forms of poison.

Snow and ice, the burning cold.
Hear the avalanche's rumbling spread;
touch of clammy skin, empty handshake.

Bleached bones to lay
in a tomb of hoary rock, gravestone to match.
The white ghost wandering.

Lifeless, emptiness,
white oblivion.

A DRAGON IN MOUNTAIN'S SHADOW

Our solemn oaths to hunt down a dragon
were made many months ago.
The day of the dragon's coming
began as any day
but ended with villages aflame.

The silent dead lay beneath red skies;
smoke drifted skyward; ash rained down.
Heart-rending songs of grief filled the air,
sung for the lost and fallen.

I was but one
of a courageous band of companions
that on that day
began a quest.

Months have since passed,
and we have traveled a distance
greater than ever before.

Today is our day,
which we have sought
these many months.

Once distant, but now within hand's reach,
a mountain ledge
rests before a cave's entrance
beneath a foreboding mountain's peak
grasping at the sun.

The valley far below-
sunshine at its heart, reflecting off autumn's leaves
and lost on flowers glowing purple, blue, and gold.

At last, it is found.
Will we succeed?
Will we return home,
to loved ones, to laughing,
to quiet sunny afternoons?

Red eyes appear in the deep darkness
of the cursed cave.
Behold, the great snake with wings;
a terror of flight, whose footsteps are earthquakes,
whose breath is death.
The Dragon.

AWAKENING

I walk on newborn blades of green,
barefoot upon Nature's flesh.
Walking
with a train of firelight at my back,
scorching nothing
but imbuing effervescent energy
that pulsates and flashes
in bright melodic waves;
it coats my skin with invisible armor;
fills my breath, my heart, my mind,
with richness striking and vast and momentary.

A feeling of all possibilities,
awaiting a single word
to be born into body and soul
and walk upon the Earth as I do.

In the night,
in the swell of adventure,
inhale the sweet
intoxicating air.
Hear the star song.
Feel the darkness open
and absorb the deep knowledge pouring out.
Know the feeling of life;
heightened senses overflowing,
expecting the answer
to the greatest question-
how to fulfill the purpose of existence.

Alive.
Can you not see
everything that shall exist
in one beating rhythm
bursting open
and pouring forth the words of Creation
and Death and Eternity.

All the same.
All in everything.

TO DREAM

I dream
of nights without end
full of daring and silver moonlight,
enthralled by blazing stars
that guide the way forever on

I dream
of enchantress' soft melodies
cradling the world
and breathing dreams of contentment and ease

I feel
waves of euphoria striking
like the bite of fruit from the Tree of Knowledge
but vanishing by the workings of the Morning Thief,
who greedily robs memories and dreams

Why do I not sleep
but hold onto the night
as the First Mother held onto the First Son?
Because all is forgotten on the morn-
oblivion of thoughts, dreams, and visions of other planes

I dream to dream
but never wake
for the dream is to be awake
and to be awake is to be the dream

I dream
to be in the space
between awake and the dream
for therein lies all;
to open my eyes and see as the Creator sees.
I dream for therein lays peace

LOVING

Our love is a kind,
like the hurricane lost at sea,
hurting no one but unyielding to man's will.
Torrid and deep as the heart of stars.
Unbreaking before all, undiminished and awe-inspiring.

The machinations of man would separate.
But they
shatter when held within our gaze,
tremble and fall away at our touch,
kneel before our words of loving
as the bud bows before the butterfly.

A GARDEN WALK

Her hand rests upon a latch,
metal and timeworn,
fashioned into the face of a bird

With a delicate push of her pale young hand,
inward groans the gate,
revealing a path carpeted by mist
that stretches into the wet, dripping green

Her footsteps without sound
on forgiving soft soil
lead her deeper and deeper
into a garden never known
by a stranger

Though cold and damp chills her skin,
her thoughts linger on the sweet garden's end.
But first a visit to make
to a seat of softened stone
holding memories of laughter
and times long since flown

It sits at the center past the roses
of dripping ruby light
and the vines and the tangles
like webs all alight,
resting beneath a canopy
of burgeoning blue light.
The tiles of marble, the statues of stone,
the mosaics with faces, unknown, unknown

A fountain propels water
over slippery smooth stone
from the heart of a mountain
born before all others known.
It is here that she drinks;
it is here that she rests
'til the hour to move on
'til a time that is soon

Then her path of mist narrows
by the strength of the starling's tune.
Its length will end at a pedestal that is waiting
on this bewitched night in June
for the woman to return,
as she is made of stone,
to stand upon the pedestal
under the light of the risen moon